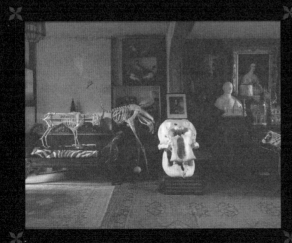

In House

In House

PHOTOGRAPHS BY

DERRY MOORE

Text By MITCHELL OWENS

RIZZOLI
NEW YORK

First published in the United States of America in 2009 by
Rizzoli International Publications, Inc.
300 Park Avenue South, New York, NY 10010
www.rizzoliusa.com

Photographs and introduction © 2009 by DERRY MOORE
Texts © 2009 by MITCHELL OWENS

2009 2010 2011 2012 / 10 9 8 7 6 5 4 3 2 1

+ Printed in Italy +

Design & Art Direction by BARNBROOK DESIGN

ISBN-13 = 978-0-8478-3349-8
ISBN-10 = 0-8478-3349-6
Library of Congress Catalog Control Number: 2009931041

✳   ✳   ✳

FOREWORD BY DERRY MOORE

::::: LONDON ::::: ENGLAND ::::: 2009 :::::

Many years ago, when Sir Humphry Wakefield showed me the ruin he had just bought that was Chillingham Castle, I was enchanted by its desolate splendour and I remember him saying, "I know that in twenty-five years you will say it was much more beautiful before I touched it." Miraculously, however, his prediction did not come true and Chillingham has retained its essence. ¶ In the selection of houses for *In House* my choice, unsurprisingly, has been influenced by the occasions where I felt happiest with the actual photographs. I have selected houses that reflect the personality of the owner or original designer, and this has involved the omission of many beautiful ones designed by professional decorators. It might be argued that this would preclude the inclusion of Alcuzcuz, the house of the distinguished Spanish decorator Jaime Parladé. However, I have included it since not only is Alcuzcuz the result of a remarkably happy collaboration between Parladé and his English wife, Janetta, but also because, above all, it is so personal, so full of paintings, furniture, and objects that are the result of years of patient collecting, and which were lovingly chosen for their individual charm or beauty. ¶ Certain other houses in this book have enjoyed the help of a professional interior designer at various stages, notably West Wycombe Park and Badminton House. Such was the sense of taste of the owners, however, and such the importance of the existing elements of these houses, that the designer's character merges into that of the house. A union like this requires a willingness on the part of the designer to refrain from asserting himself at the expense of the house – a sort of professional humility. When that is lacking, although the result may be interesting and stimulating, it doesn't always succeed in complementing the intrinsic nature of the house. An example of this type of designer would be the late David Hicks. He had a magnificent boldness in his approach to the most established house but reticence is not the adjective that springs to mind when describing his work. Another great designer, David Mlinaric, would certainly qualify as the supreme contemporary proponent of the more sympathetic approach and with great justification he was the principal designer for the National Trust – houses such as Beningborough, Nostell Priory, and Ashdown House have been meticulously restored by him for the Trust, not to mention his remarkable work at Spencer House in London and the Royal Opera House, both veritable tours de force; the latter having been totally gutted in the 1990s now looks as if it has not been touched since it was built 150 years previously.

In this book there are various categories that frequently overlap and the only quality that I hope is constant is an element of surprise – by which I do not mean necessarily places that were merely bizarre. There are those houses that were designed in one fell swoop, so to speak, such as Houghton or Sidi Bou Said, where the original design was so rigorous that any later additions would have seemed superfluous, just as mistletoe is not missed when it is removed from the tree on which it grows. Then there are the houses such as Badminton House and West Wycombe Park, both of which have had the advantage of inheriting superb collections of furniture and paintings. These houses, bearing the additions and modifications of successive owners, have acquired a rich patina over the years. There are also those places such as Kinloch Castle on the Isle of Rum, which for whatever reason have been abandoned, rather like the palace in *Sleeping Beauty*, with spiders and mice – and moths, alas! – the only tenants. Malplaquet House in London, is of particular interest, since although the individual objects and pieces of furniture – collected magpie-like by the owners – are not in themselves exceptional in quality, yet the overall effect is one of a slightly faded grandeur. It is as if a brilliant sleight of hand had been performed, leaving the visitor intrigued and enchanted without knowing precisely why. ¶ Most of the houses in this book express the desire for some perfected and unspecified, even unconscious ideal. A supreme example of this is Chillingham Castle in the wilds of Northumberland, a classic example of one man's vision, of an almost quixotic wish to create an ancestral home within a few years – and succeeding. ¶ This yearning for an ideal is the prime motivation in the creation of many great houses, almost an expression of the desire for immortality – a more practical expression than that of some popes who commissioned their own extravagant tombs during their lifetimes. It is certainly evident in Sir John Soane's London house, built by him at the end of the eighteenth century and now a museum. Although Soane is generally described as a classical architect, and although in its design his house is eminently practical and innovative, how romantic his collection is! Each object in that extraordinary place would have conjured up not just memories but visions and ideas for its remarkable owner. The lighting – daylight, of course – involves hidden skylights and an extensive and completely original use of mirrors, and is of such subtlety and harmony that scarcely any additional lighting was required when I photographed it.

Rooms generally acquire
an added glow when the sun enters, and
most lose that special lustre when it departs – rather as
the magic vanishes in a theatre, when the stage lighting is switched
off and the scene is once again lit only by the dull glimmer of the house
lights. Indeed, with the glow of reflected sunshine a quite humdrum room will
sometimes look better in a photograph than a more beautiful one without that glow.
Even on the dullest day, however, the rooms in the Soane Museum retain their charm and
mystery. ¶ Poor quality of light was not a problem when photographing Patrick Leigh Fermor's
house, surrounded as it is by the blinding light of the Peloponnese. Built by himself and his wife
with the help of a local workforce and completed a few years previously, this house had already in
1985 the atmosphere of somewhere that had existed for a hundred years – doubtless helped by the
owner's cats, animals that Leigh Fermor describes as the best "downholsterers." ¶ It is interesting
to consider what ingredients go to make a successful room, a room that one wants to linger in, since
we all have different criteria. Some people like a room to be cluttered, whereas others may complain
of claustrophobia in that same space. Some like large, relatively empty rooms, others small intimate
ones; some like books to browse in and pictures to look at, while others have little interest in such
things – I have noticed, incidentally, that professional decorators are rarely interested in pictures
and works of art for their own sake, but rather as elements in the general scheme of a room. Perhaps
the answer to this conundrum of what the necessary ingredients are for a successful room might be
found in the reply to the question as to what made the cassoulet so delicious – was it the sausage,
was it the pork, the beans, the herbs? – the answer being quite simply, the cook! ¶ A room that looks
appealing in a photograph, however, may not necessarily be a pleasant one in which to live. There are
many elements that contribute to a room's success from a photographic point of view; apart from the
paramount one of the light and how it falls, there is the question of the arrangement of the furniture
and whether it will look right in the photograph – will that sofa in the foreground overwhelm
everything else, will the owner's favourite cushion with the coy quotation attract too much attention,
ditto the lampshade – and whether everything will appear in proportion on the page as it does to
the eye, which makes suitable adjustments for the mind. The rooms that present most problems are
generally dining rooms and bedrooms, the former having the inconvenient presence of the dining
room table, the latter of the bed, both of which in a photograph have a tendency to overwhelm their
settings. To say that the camera doesn't lie is itself a lie and the art of the photographer consists
largely in making it lie in such a way as to capture the essence of a room. What I hope is that the
photographs in this book might encourage its readers to see places with a fresh eye and to discover
that what they had hitherto taken for granted had its own particular beauty and mystery.

**************** ///////////////////////////// 1 0 + 11 —— > _____ :::::::::::::::::::::
::: *** :::::::::::
:: _____ ::::::::::::: /////////// :::::::::::::::::::::::::::::

INDEX *of*

HOUSES

∧ ∧ ∧

Malplaquet House

LONDON ○ ENGLAND ○ 2005

The museum curator Tim Knox and the landscape architect
Todd Longstaffe-Gowan have a finely tuned fascination
with the dead. Whether it is a towering chimneypiece
ornamented with a human skull or a death mask of Napoleon,
few exceptional examples of memento mori escape their
appreciative grasp. Even the name of the couple's 1742 house
in London, Malplaquet House, refers to a graveyard of
sorts – the devastating battle of Malplaquet in 1709, the
bloodiest conflict of the eighteenth century. By the time the
men discovered the four-story townhouse in the city's East End
it was fairly lifeless, having been undermined by more than
a century of neglect and a well-aimed bomb during the Blitz.

::::::::::::::: (1 6 + 1 7) _____ * * *
_____ :::::::::::::::::::::::::: >>>>>>>//////////

THE ONLY TRUE LIKENESS OF OUR SAVIOUR.

Today the marks of centuries of change and disregard have
been carefully preserved and its twenty-odd rooms outfitted
with bizarre curiosities. A replica of an Egyptian mummy case
stands in the Sarcophagus Room. In the Picture Room, doleful
antique portraits of nuns look down upon the skeletal remains
of an ostrich and a regiment of animal skulls. An immense
tiger pelt is draped over a sofa, and a stuffed mountain goat
lies underneath a table loaded with Victorian marble busts.
An image of the Virgin is sketched onto the dried skin of a
chicken (the artist's name, appropriately enough, is Strange)
and a blood-flecked Christ, wrought in Victorian stained glass,
is propped next to the kitchen stove. ¶ Not everything speaks of
the netherworld, however. As hawk-eyed as they are knowingly
macabre, Knox and Longstaffe-Gowan have dotted their
home with some real treasures within and without – including
an astounding unfinished portrait by Sir Anthony van Dyck
and a walled garden planted with towering ferns that lend an
unexpectedly Amazonian touch to this corner of Stepney.

>>>>>>> ////////// :::::::::::::::: _____^
::::::: _____ +++++ ::::::::::::::: (2 2 + 2 3)

HOC ERAT IN VOTIS. MODUS AGRI NON ITA MAGNUS.
HORTUS UBI ET TECTO VICINUS JUGIS AQUÆ FONS.
ET PAULUM SILVÆ SUPER HIS FORET, AUCTIUS ATQUE
DI MELIUS FECERE. BENE EST. NIHIL AMPLIUS ORO..

KARDAMYLI

PELOPONNESE ◦ GREECE ◦ 1986

ebrated travel writer Sir Patrick Leigh Fermor
n eventful life. A traveler – and during World
I a highly distinguished soldier – he walked
urope at the age of nineteen and saw himself
yed on screen in 1957 by Dirk Bogarde, who
d his part in the abduction of a Nazi general
pied Crete. It seems only natural, then, that
ermor would have desired a peaceful respite.
ly 1960s, he moved to what was then a largely
d area of Greece, seduced by a painterly vista
y green islands and glittering aquamarine sea
n now seem to await the return of Odysseus.
mor describes this stretch of the Peloponnese
ner's Greece," and the house he and his wife,
designed for themselves and completed in
ves the impression of having existed here for

generations. ¶ Elegantly proportioned yet no more
complicated than a child's drawing, the low-slung
structure near the village of Kardamyli is "a rambling
peasant house, with huge airy rooms," Leigh Fermor
has observed, built amid an olive grove at the foot
of "a great amphitheatre of mountains which turn a
hectic red at sunset." Chunks of pale golden limestone,
carried to the hilly site on the backs of mules, make
up its rough-hewn walls; the weathered red-clay roof
tiles were salvaged from buildings damaged in an
earthquake. The latest generation of cats, which have
reproduced on the property for decades – "Joan hasn't
the heart to chuck them in the briny, so here we are,"
Leigh Fermor wrote in mock despair to his friend the
Duchess of Devonshire – slink in and out of the cool
white rooms, slumbering on a massive banquette in

pools of sunlight or darting past a large round
table that bears the image of the sun in inlaid m
¶ The residence of a scholar, the house's wide-
contents bear witness to a curious mind and far
journeys. Beneath the living room's basketwe
pattern wood ceiling are hundreds of books by a
ranging from Proust to Bruce Chatwin, and o
mantelpiece are displayed pieces of Attic pott
unpretentious hodgepodge of furniture old and
arranged on gray stone floors: Greek Revival ma
chairs, simple low pine tables with carpenter-
silhouettes, and a Victorian easy chair upholste
the colorful remains of an antique kilim. Outc
pebbled terraces edged with plain slab benche
a panorama of sea and sky that remains unalt
since the day Leigh Fermor first saw it.

Belkis Hanim Yali

When one looks across the sparkling waters of the Bosphorus from the European side to the Asiatic, the eye is drawn to the eighteenth-century seaside mansion known as Belkis Hanim Yali on account of the intensity of its unexpected complexion. A deep red stain coats the wooden exterior, the startling shade intensified by the contrast of the deep green trees and rare shrubs brought from the Caucasus mountains more than 100 years ago by a wealthy pasha. The interiors, however, of this elegant house in the hilly Salacak quarter of Istanbul – its name means the Villa of Lady Belkis, recalling its most renowned resident, the pasha's daughter, a woman whose odalisque beauty mesmerized Turkey in the 1920s – are pale and luminous. The chalky whites, dusty pinks, and sky blues, combined with expansive windows and balconies positioned to take advantage of refreshing sea breezes, provide a welcome escape from the hot, humid city center in summer. Sunlight reflecting off the strait that separates the Asian and European sides of Istanbul seeps through delicate fretwork panels and dapples the creamy walls with a gentle aqueous glow. ¶ Nuri Birgi, a distinguished statesman who served as the Turkish ambassador to the Court of St. James as well as its envoy to NATO, acquired the leaky and collapsing landmark in 1968 from the elderly Belkis Hanim and spent the next three years meticulously restoring it in concert with Turgut Cansever, the country's leading architect. Some of the pasha's embellishments, added in the 1890s and deemed too fussily Victorian, were scraped away, but others were preserved – notably applied moldings that give the ceilings a coffered appearance, as well as high-relief carved tulips and other stylized flowers that bloom along the top of a paneled chair rail. In keeping with its status as an informal retreat built by the water's edge, the *yali's* furnishings are few and relatively simple. In the living room, plain wooden sofas contrast with Louis XV-style tabourets, all crisply lacquered white and upholstered in nougat-colored fabrics. Modern square ottomans in two shades of blue velvet are placed in a columned room used for receptions. The broad windows are bare, except for the modest white blinds. Strips of sisal are laid across the wood floors, its golden tone and rough corrugation relieved by Anatolian carpets, their brilliant colors softened by time. Candy-striped spheres of Venetian glass – red-and-white in the living room, blue-and-white in Birgi's tree-shaded study – serve as doorknobs. Underscoring the maritime setting are dashes of sapphire and aquamarine that come from the ambassador's collection of antique vessels, shaped like giant teardrops and designed to hold rosewater. As a result, the atmosphere of this beautiful house is a surprising blend of solemnity and refreshment, clarity and complication.

Alcuzcuz

For the home of so revered an interior decorator, Jaime Parladé's earth-red hacienda in southern Spain is more haphazardly organic than rigidly organized. Its colorful mélange of patterns and periods reflects the harmonious collaboration between the refined eye of the Andalusian gentleman and the relaxed style of his English artist wife, Janetta, a longtime friend of Francis Bacon, John Craxton, and Lucien Freud.

<<< ------ <> -------------------- < < < < < < < < < < > > > > > > -------------------------------- <<<

Although it retains the original exterior of an undistinguished stucco farmhouse, reconstructed in Spanish baroque fashion fifty-odd years ago and crowned by a shapely bell tower, the Parladés' house is a multicultural hybrid in whose rooms Iberian, Arabic, and English influences blend in equal, easygoing measure – much like Jaime Parladé himself, who grew up in Tangiers. Encased in heavy frames, portraits of grandees and their ladies share rooms with tribal kilims woven in dusty shades of orange and madder red and relics of Victorian days such as needlework slipper chairs. A pair of Georgian canopy beds is unexpectedly paired with exotic silk hangings fit for a caïd's palace. Another bed hosts a surprisingly mismatched wardrobe – a patchwork coverlet of vaguely African mien, a boldly graphic Moroccan appliqué panel, a skirt of flowered English linen, as well as a striped wool throw resembling a handsome saddle blanket and a length of textile that appears to be a tasseled remnant of Turkish carpet.

<<<<< --- >>>>> -------------------------------- < < < < < < ----- <<<<< ------------

The result is an atmosphere that is both worldly and unpretentious, with its contents seemingly acquired over time and arranged with uncommon grace. In the entrance hall an antique paisley shawl is spread across the top of a modest wood table set with a porcelain jug filled with rosy oleander blossoms and a handmade ceramic lamp whose silhouette is charmingly lopsided. Elsewhere a nineteenth-century sofa upholstered in French toile de Jouy has been placed against a wainscot of polychrome tiles, and in the living room a button-tufted Napoléon III *borne* is positioned beneath a ceiling fan that lazily turns, stirring the still Spanish air.

CASINO DE MADRID

MADRID ✦ SPAIN ✦ 1982

Though the limestone exterior of the Casino de Madrid is a relatively sober affair, the interior of this private gentlemen's club is all operatic frosting and folderol. Domed, chandeliered, muraled, gilded, sculpted, peppered with stained glass, and laced with wrought iron, its palatial rooms seem less acts of architecture than triumphs of the pastry chef's art. The confectionery extravagance – described by one visitor as "Rococo Vienna/ Würzburg as re-created in Second Empire Paris with extra geegaws" – is so complicated that it comes as little surprise to learn that this meticulously restored relic of Edwardian Spain is not the work of one architect or even one firm. Unable to choose between half a dozen outstanding entries submitted by leading Beaux-Arts practitioners in an international competition in 1903, the club's board of directors simply combined the favored plans into one grandiose structure, erecting what remains the Spanish capital's most august watering hole.

Photographing the Casino de Madrid was Derry Moore's introduction to Spanish buildings of the period. Having previously imagined that Gaudi was an isolated phenomenon, this building revealed that he derived from a tradition that was an idiosyncratic interpretation of Art Nouveau. The vaulted library is characterized by neo-Gothic solemnity, while the Salón Real, a vast ballroom flooded with natural light, enriched by chubby plaster cherubs, and with romantic landscapes decorating its ceiling, is a Ruritanian-style setting in search of an operetta. The most majestic feature of the building, which served as a hospital during the Spanish Civil War before falling into disrepair under the Franco dictatorship, is a double staircase that swirls up through the entrance hall, its snow-white marble looking as weightless as meringue.

(54 + 55)

YESTER HOUSE

· EAST LOTHIAN · SCOTLAND · 2008 ·

Arguably the most beautiful house in Scotland and containing an eighteenth-century saloon of sublime proportions and refined stucco ornamentation which has been acclaimed for more than two centuries as the country's finest room, Yester House remains strangely little known. The cumulative work of several geniuses – including father-and-son architects William and Robert Adam, who remodeled the seventeenth-century mansion near Edinburgh for the 4th Marquess of Tweeddale – it is severe in effect but surprisingly quirky in its details, a compelling mélange of Baroque, Rococo, and Neoclassical influences. The roof of the east pavilion, for example, is as curvaceous as a teapot's lid, while Robert Adam's garden entrance rises an impressive three stories, its urn-topped pediment and Ionic pilasters lending the stone-and-brick building the sleepy spirit of a gracious Italian estate. ¶ This Italianate accent could be one reason that the composer and founder of the Spoleto festival, Gian Carlo Menotti – dubbed Mr. McNotty by local villagers – and his son, Francis, chose to live at Yester House for more than thirty-five years. As a result its rooms have long been enriched with music, from the sound of a quartet navigating a new composition to an opera singer scaling one or another of Menotti's arias. The dramatic air of the interiors makes a perfect background, the theatrical furnishings and unexpected juxtapositions of scale a reflection of the owners' artistic vocations. A modern Lucite table in Menotti's study is topped with Chinese porcelain; the windows of a sulphur-yellow drawing room are crowned by neo-Gothic valances trimmed with oversized scarlet tassels. In the composer's study, an Italian organ case – painted celestial blue and decorated with giltwood angels – is reinvented as a palatial bookcase. At the heart of Yester House is the admired saloon, whose thirty-foot-high ceiling is set with myriad octagonal stucco medallions and rosettes, and whose walls display enormous classical murals, their bucolic scenes echoed in the wooded Lammermuir hills that roll gently beyond the room's arched windows – the same hills, appropriately enough, that provide the setting for Donizetti's opera *Lucia di Lammermoor*.

(((::: +++++)))

\\\\\\\\\\\\\ ::::: 70 + 71 :::::::::::::::::::::::

::::::::::::::::::::::::::::::::::::::: //////////////

Sir John Soane's Museum

LONDON ::: ENGLAND ::: 2008

"The Soane Museum is as deep as St. Paul's dome is wide," an admirer once wrote with good reason. The treasure of Lincoln's Inn Fields in London, this intricate and eccentric townhouse, created between 1792 and 1824 by the architect Sir John Soane, is one man's unique experiment in shaping space. A triumph of both spatial invention and catholic collecting instincts, the building melds three adjoining structures into a five-floor repository of the strange, the fine, and the unique. Like a discerning magpie, John Soane, a renegade neoclassicist, filled dozens of ingeniously remodeled rooms with thousands of objects, deliberately arranging his finds into a three-dimensional jigsaw puzzle intended to educate and inspire. ¶ Arranged today as they were nearly two centuries ago, the flotsam and jetsam of different cultures are balanced on brackets and shelves: marble busts of British worthies, imposing Roman cinerary urns, and a significant chunk of the Parthenon's frieze are all dramatically displayed. Hidden skylights send down shafts of milky illumination, and cleverly placed mirrors distribute the light with extraordinary care and originality. Scores of paintings by William Hogarth are hung on hinged wall panels that fold open to reveal yet another layer of works by other artists. Medieval stained glass, reportedly removed from monasteries razed during the French Revolution, join paintings by Canaletto, the sarcophagus of Pharaoh Seti I, and architectural models—including one depicting the façade of Soane's remarkable design of the Bank of England, arguably the masterpiece of his long career and now sadly demolished. ¶ The total effect is dizzying, a mosaic of sublime acquisitiveness. "Every inch of space, every corner, every bit of wall is literally 'stuck over' with scraps and odds and ends of sculptures and fragments," a bedazzled reporter wrote in *Tinsley's Magazine* in 1884, nearly eighty years after Soane first opened his house to students of the Royal Academy, where he served as professor of architecture. "All seems to have been as fish to the owner's net."

PAINTINGS ON SILK.......(LABELLE)

Château de Pesselières

SANCERRE · FRANCE · 2001

A French muralist and sculptor influenced by such disparate move-
ments as the Gothic Revival, 1930s Surrealism, and pharaonic Egypt,
Paulin Pâris treats his country house as if it were a constantly evolving
canvas. So restless is his imagination, the fancies seen here may well
by now have already vanished, obscured beneath other whimsies.
Although it has been modified by centuries of owners, most of the
house dates from the twelfth century; but the artful interiors of the
Château de Pesselières in the French canton of Sancerre are a glossary
of imaginative designs that offer striking counterpoints to those
unrenovated sections of the castle distinguishable by worn parquet
and crumbling plaster. ¶ A mural depicting Venetian-style arches can be
seen on the perimeter of the artist's office, each trompe l'oeil opening
softened by equally trompe red curtains. Golden quatrefoils speckle
the scarlet walls of the dining room, the repeating pattern occasionally
broken by large imitation tapestries of canvas loosely tacked into place
and enlivened by bosky scenes – a medieval maiden languishing in the
shade of wizened trees, a baroque fountain overlooked by a trelliswork
arbor. In the immense room that has now been transformed into a
Spartan bath, Pâris coated the plaster walls with a constellation of
pale hieroglyphics suggesting a synthesis of Chagall and Cocteau.
The kitchen remains as yet unimproved by the artist's lyrical brush,
evocative of a different age, its old walls cracked and stained and five
barley-twist chairs arranged beneath the glassy stare of deers' heads.

Hôtel Masseran

Decoratively speaking, *le goût Rothschild* is usually understood to describe lofty rooms of Second Empire opulence, awash in gauffrage velvet and bullion fringe and seasoned with Old Master paintings, Boulle cabinets, and rare Renaissance bronzes. But two members of this famous European banking dynasty largely eschewed the family's traditionally operatic style in favor of restrained neoclassicism — albeit by way of the Palais de Versailles. Despite this stylistic detour, the look espoused by Liliane and Elie de Rothschild, part owners of the Palais Lafite Rothschild vineyard, was no less luxurious, thanks to its fine bureau plats, giltwood tabourets, and delicately carved boiseries hung with portraits of eminences of the ancien régime. ¶ Married by proxy during World War II — at the time, the baron was being held as a prisoner of war in Germany — the couple and their three children eventually settled in a stately *hôtel particulier* at 11 rue Masseran in Paris. Built in 1787 by architect Alexandre-Théodore Brongniart, Hôtel Masseran had long been the home of Count Étienne de Beaumont, a flamboyant twentieth-century patron of

the avant-garde arts who designed jewels for Christian Dior and choreographed ballets when he wasn't hosting costume balls. Tastemaker Eugenia Errázuriz lived there too, occupying one of its pavilions courtesy of Beaumont and his wife. The Rothschilds, however, adopted a quieter position in society and after purchasing the house from the count in 1956, they furnished it with a lavish period decor that gave the storied property's public rooms a museum-like air. ¶ The baroness in particular was drawn to objects and literature associated with Marie Antoinette, a scholarly fascination that resulted in her becoming a discreet but powerful presence in the preservation and authentic refurbishment of the Château de Versailles. That the Hôtel Masseran was built for Prince Masserano, a cousin of Louis XVI, surely contributed to its attraction to its historically-minded twentieth-century chatelaine. (The vast pilastered salon, long considered a magnificent example of eighteenth-century craftsmanship, was actually a cunning reproduction created more than 100 years later.) The baroness's admiration of the noble past doubtless

inspired her to furnish the rooms of the house with rare Aubusson carpets, tortoiseshell cabinets, and *fauteuils à la reine* made by ébénistes patronized by the French court during the reigns of Louis XV and Louis XVI. ¶ The splendor was appropriate enough; an editor of French *Vogue* considered the Rothschilds "the true successors of the Bourbons in France." The rich array of objects included many that had belonged to Marie Antoinette, one being the queen's red velvet purse. Liliane de Rothschild was a determined collector and rarely did anything she desired escape her manicured grasp; as she said of one costly purchase, "I wanted to buy it at any price, and at that price I got it." The art the couple acquired over the years was a bit more adventuresome and included works by Picasso and Dubuffet as well as Rembrandt's *The Standard-Bearer*. One masterpiece after the next found its home so successfully in the densely furnished Hôtel Masseran over the decades that a Rothschild biographer observed of the baroness, "Some pieces she absorbs so well that, rumor goes, they are never seen again."

Geraldine
Thomsen-Muchová

+ PRAGUE + CZECH REPUBLIC + 1984 +

In the Prague apartment of the composer Geraldine Thomsen-Muchová, a previous generation's eclectic taste reigns. Renaissance Revival chairs, an oval Victorian cheval glass, and marble-top tables in the style of Louis XV alternate with paintings of impassive beauties framed by lush white flowers. Filled with belongings that once furnished a much larger villa, it is a shrine to a man she never met, her father-in-law, the Art Nouveau artist Alfons Mucha, his belongings now preserved within the confines of a few worn rooms inside a handsome eighteenth-century palace at the foot of Prague Castle. A faded photograph of Mucha and his friend Paul Gauguin shows the two artists in their underwear gleefully playing a mahogany harmonium. The same harmonium is here in the salon, set against an eighteenth-century Baroque mural, the instrument's dark, shining surface supporting the unlikely juxtaposition of a crucifix and an African figurine. Mucha's drawings, paintings, and posters dominate the cramped interiors, and certain personal belongings – an empty tin of the Player's Navy Cut cigarettes the artist smoked, a stuffed bird that was used as a prop in his studio, scores of family photographs – are reverently preserved, tucked in wherever space can be found, all assembled into a mosaic of century-old memories illumined by sunlight from Hradčanské Square.

HOUGHTON HALL

NORFOLK ::: ENGLAND ::: 1997

Houghton Hall, the seat
of the Marquesses of Cholmondeley,
rises above Norfolk's flat, gray-green landscape,
an unchallenged declaration of the majesty of English
Palladianism. Its high central block, curving colonnades,
and low flaring wings are a perfectly symmetrical tribute to the
wealth, power, and patronage of Sir Robert Walpole, simultaneously
First Lord of the Treasury and Chancellor of the Exchequer, a man whose
consolidation of power during the reigns of George I and George II resulted
in his being considered the country's first prime minister. Loathed and admired
in equal measure for his political dominance and astute fortune building—John
Gay lampooned him as the avaricious character Bob Booty in *The Beggar's
Opera*—Walpole intended the house to glorify the dynasty he intended to father.
So in an inspired alliance with Colen Campbell, the most interesting architect
of his day and author of *Vitruvius Britannicus*, the architect James Gibbs, and the
designer William Kent, Walpole transformed his family's outmoded Jacobean house
into a luxurious palace whose marble chambers, glittering Baroque furniture, and
astounding art collection (the debts of a later generation resulting in the sale of
nearly half the collection to Catherine the Great) were deemed "incredibly vulgar
and over-the-top" in the 1720s—as the present Lord Cholmondeley, descendent
of Walpole, has observed. ¶ Distance, however, lends enchantment, and details
that appeared nouveau riche in Houghton's heyday now seem to be matchless
expressions of Palladianism at its most robust. Pairs of cherubs recline on the
pedimented doorcases of the terraced stone hall, whose great plasterwork swags
and frieze of impassive lion heads were made by the Italian plasterer Giuseppe
Artari. A gilt-framed ceiling mural sparkles above a state bed designed by William
Kent and covered in rich green velvet, the oversized shell-shaped headboard
trimmed with intricate silver galloon darkened by time. The central staircase rises
in stately fashion, floor by shadowed floor, its broad wood handrail passing trompe
l'oeil medallions and grotesques accented with gold leaf. Outdoors, balustraded
terraces command painterly views of the park and the estate's peculiar white fallow
deer. Walpole's descendants—though they briefly flirted with selling the estate in
the late nineteenth century—have ensured that their progenitor's creation remains
undimmed; notably Sybil Cholmondeley, the present marquess's grandmother, who
devoted her long life to restoring the house's glory. Imposing and monumental,
Houghton Hall is an aristocratic gesture in the peaceful Norfolk countryside.

West Wycombe Park

———————— BUCKINGHAMSHIRE | ENGLAND | 1997 ————————

With pedimented façades that replicate ancient temples, ceilings frescoed with mythological scenes of bare-breasted gods and goddesses, and a monumental entrance hall forested with thick columns and modeled after a Roman atrium, West Wycombe Park is a setting destined to encourage personal excesses. Until his death in 2000, Sir Francis Dashwood, the 11th baronet, was fond of donning curly-toed shoes and a turban during costume parties at this Buckinghamshire country house – an outfit, as Derry Moore affectionately observed, which more closely resembled the uniform of a doorman at an Indian restaurant than the authentic dress of the subcontinent. ¶ In the eighteenth century, Sir Francis's ancestor and namesake, the 2nd baronet, was portrayed wearing the dress of a friar in his role as founder of the Brotherhood of St. Francis of Wycombe, a pagan association whose notorious erotic entertainments led it to be called the Hell-Fire Club. However, when Sir Francis wasn't hosting orgies in the estate's underground caverns, the eighteenth-century libertine rebuilt the family's uninteresting Carolean seat in spectacular neoclassical fashion. One of the many enlightened gentlemen of his day to be influenced by the sixteenth-century Italian architect Andrea Palladio, Dashwood remodeled West Wycombe in the manner of a villa in the Veneto. Stretched across the south façade was a 300-foot-long loggia constructed with nearly thirty Tuscan and Corinthian columns, with brooding stone busts set on plinths and a large plaster cast of the Borghese Hermaphrodite. The interiors were furnished with equal panache and included a second-century Roman sarcophagus, walls painted to resemble giant blocks of semiprecious jasper, and rare tapestries cut to fit around doors and windows. ¶ By the 1940s, the former splendor of West Wycombe Park had dimmed, and a visiting diplomat regretfully observed that the house was "in a state of … disrepair, peeling statues with their noses knocked off, holes on the drive." The Dashwood of the day, Sir John, despised the place and turned the ravishing King's Room into a modern kitchen, ripping out its elaborate architectural details and whitewashing its frescoes. He also sold off hundreds of the house's treasures, leaving it to his heir, the future turban-wearer, to spend decades tracking down the discarded Queen Anne walnut chairs and Persian works of art in a lifelong quest to revive West Wycombe Park's late-Georgian glory. Largely successful in his endeavor, today only one major original furnishing remains at large – the state bed topped with giltwood pineapples, reportedly designed by Thomas Chippendale and sold in the 1920s for just fifty-eight pounds.

WASTE NOT,   WANT NOT.

ERDDIG HALL

WREXHAM + WALES + 1982

Paintings of lords and ladies populate many a British country house, gazing across history in powdered wigs and silk petticoats. At Erddig Hall in north Wales, however, portraits of servants outnumber portraits of Yorkes, the family that inherited the stern, neoclassical stone mansion in the eighteenth century, living amidst and contributing to its sedimentary layers for more than 200 years (they seem never to have thrown anything away). Although the main rooms at Erddig are filled with stately-home furnishings—a Gainsborough depicting the first Philip Yorke, sauce tureens by master silversmith Paul de Lamerie, a bedchamber hung with Chinese Export wallpaper—it is what lies downstairs that makes this Denbighshire house so unusual, and which explains why visitors today are greeted at the modest service entrance rather than at the grand front door. ¶ One of the family's eccentric traditions was to commission paintings and photographs of its servants—cooks, grooms, blacksmiths, gamekeepers, and other staff members, all of whom "bestow their toil on this estate!" as one early Yorke declared—and then hang them on the distempered walls of the servants' hall and adjacent corridors, the tools of each subject's trade proudly in hand and the canvases daubed with whimsical verses praising his or her steadfast loyalty and occupational expertise. The carpenter Thomas Rogers is captured for eternity in his sawdusted workshop, looking up from his labors with a slightly surprised expression on his clean-shaven face, as if interrupted by a question from the master of the day. Dressed in red-and-blue livery, an unnamed black youth cradles a brass hunting horn while a poetic epitaph extolling his virtues unfurls alongside, hoping his spirit resides in Heaven, "Where black or white/Distinctions end/For sure on this side of the grave/They are too strong, tw'ixt Lord and Slave." Thomas Pritchard, a weathered gardener, is recorded in oil tending a patch of luxuriant flora. Funereal diamond-shaped plaques honor the service of aged butlers, and numerous Victorian black-and-white photographs depict Erddig's household staff lined up on its front steps in the manner of schoolchildren assembled for a class picture. A painting of Edward Barnes, a forester who also brewed the thousand-acre estate's beer in the 1830s, is shown strolling along a wooded path, an axe resting on one strong shoulder and a lively spaniel trotting at his heels. Nevertheless, there were limits to the Yorkes' unusual admiration for their domestic help. As one lady of the house indignantly informed her son and heir in the 1760s, her personal maid was indeed a talented artist but the young woman's brush needed to be stilled, otherwise "I shall have no service from her & make too fine a Lady of her, for so much say'd on that occasion that it rather puffs her up."

BADMINTON

Badminton, in Gloucestershire, the home of the Somerset family since 1608, achieved its present form in the early eighteenth century. The existing Jacobean house was redesigned in a more contemporary form by the third Duke of Beaufort, a descendant of Edward III. He engaged some of the most important designers of the day, including the architects William Kent and James Gibbs, and the wood-carver Grinling Gibbons, to remodel what was perceived as an old-fashioned structure. Such was the success of the renovation of the house (the huge entrance hall is reportedly the birthplace of the sport that takes the house's name) and grounds that the duke's close neighbors, it was said, landscaped their own properties to appear like a continuation of the Badminton estate. The splendor of the place, combined with its remoteness from London, was such that at the outbreak of the Second World War in 1939, it was deemed to be the safest and most appropriate retreat for Queen Mary, mother of King George VI. ¶ A year after the 11th Duke of Beaufort and his late wife, Caroline, moved into Badminton in 1984, they had humanized its majesty; plants and flowers softened the grandeur of the library, created in the mid-nineteenth century by Jeffry Wyatville, and in the great drawing room, photographs of the fox-hunting duke in mid-gallop were arranged on the antique consoles. White slipcovers stenciled in red with the scrolled Beaufort monogram brightened a dining room hung with portraits of Elizabethan ancestors. The Duke and Duchess's lively approach to living at Badminton brought a welcome informality to the house. "Chairs are for sitting on, so sit on all of them," the Duchess was known to exhort tourists, regardless of the seats' condition or provenance, "and take as many photographs as you like."

KINLOCH CASTLE

Every century has moments of opulence, though few have been quite so luxurious as that brief, shining post-Victorian period, the Edwardian era, named after Edward VII, a monarch fond of indulgence and good living. The nouveaux riches of early twentieth-century Britain played out their pampered lives in extravagant new mansions designed for entertaining on an imperial scale. One of the most telling survivors of that hedonistic whirl of discreet liaisons and shooting parties is Kinloch Castle, at the head of Loch Scresort on the remote Hebridean island of Rum. ¶ Completed in 1901 at the dawn of the king's reign, Kinloch is a turreted country house decorated in the then-fashionable Scots Baronial style for Sir George Bullough, a sportsman and cavalry officer enriched by the manufacture of textile-industry equipment. The castellation of Kinloch gives Sir George's lakeside retreat the romantic roofline of a fortification out of one of Sir Walter Scott's novels, but the immense loggia wrapping three sides of the rugged, red-sandstone edifice hints at far less martial pursuits. So also do the richly decorated interiors, the now faded yet still remarkably complete schemes that blend Sir George's preference for fashionable Gothic gloom – he kept alligators as pets, while his wife kept hummingbirds in the conservatory – with the gold damask and white-painted Empire furniture favored by Monica Bullough, whom he married two years after Kinloch was built. The daughter of a French marquis, the glamorous Lady Bullough claimed, without any convincing evidence, a family connection to the Bonapartes, though that lack of genealogical proof did not stop her from installing a drawing room designed in the manner of Percier and Fontaine. ¶ During its brief heyday between its completion and the 1920s, Kinloch was used only a few weeks each year – with guests shuttled to the Bulloughs' private island by train and the Bullough steam yacht – before being largely shuttered after Sir George's death in 1939, which explains its full complement of evocative relics. Lady Bullough sold the house in 1957 and though the castle has since been used as a hotel, many of its contents remain, from snooker cues and telegraph pads to volumes of sheet music, stacked on the Steinway grand piano in the grand hall, each bound in red leather and bearing Monica Bullough's monogram in gold. Embedded in a paneled wall near the smoking room is a rare orchestrion, a large steam-powered electric organ that plays popular pieces of the time such as the *William Tell Overture* and *Home, Sweet Home* with all the sounds of a forty-piece orchestra. These and other souvenirs elevate Kinloch Castle from a millionaire baronet's costly plaything to an evocative symbol of a bygone era.

CLAYTON

~~~~~~~~~~~~ PITTSBURGH + UNITED STATES + 1989 ~~~~~~~~~~~~

Although Henry Clay Frick, the coke and steel magnate, moved to New York City and erected a Louis XVI-style palace in 1914, his old-fashioned redbrick mansion in Pittsburgh remained an emotional anchor. There he and his wife, Adelaide, raised three children, including Frick's favorite daughter, Martha, who died aged six in 1891. Little more than a decade later the house, known as Clayton in an adaptation of his middle name, was largely shuttered, encased in the amber of sentiment as the family shifted its home base.

The Fricks' fiercely loyal daughter Helen, however, who relished her role as the guardian of her father's memory, made Clayton her legal residence and spent part of each year living there. So much did she favor it over the grand Fifth Avenue establishment, a well-worn tale goes, that her dog was trained to play dead when she said "New York," and to leap when it heard her utter the word "Pittsburgh." ¶ Miss Frick ensured that Clayton's overstuffed, dust-gathering opulence – precisely the kind of interiors loathed by Elsie de Wolfe, the Francophile decorator her father hired to furnish much of his Manhattan mansion – remained largely unspoiled by modern intrusions. Lace-trimmed tea gowns, detachable collars, carriages, melodramatic Barbizon and French Academy paintings, even patent medicines – all were preserved as sacred emblems of earlier, perhaps happier times. After Miss Frick's death in 1984 this determined rejection of the twentieth century (Helen Frick famously refused women wearing trousers access to the Frick art-reference library) turned out to be preservation's blessing, when Clayton underwent restoration before being opened as a museum. In several rooms, little had to be altered, since the property had been reverently maintained as a living time capsule, right down to the telephones installed in 1883 and still used by the lady of the house and her servants more than a century later.

Rodmarton House

GLOUCESTERSHIRE ::: ENGLAND ::: 1989

The commission of a family home for Margaret and Claud Biddulph, a newly married English couple, was less the fulfillment of a private dream than the flowering of a public works project. Rather than propose an extravagant manor in the fashion of contemporaries similarly buoyed by a considerable fortune, the Biddulphs and their architect, Ernest Barnsley, planned a house on the edge of Rodmarton, a small village in the distant Cotswolds, which would be a radical celebration of the Arts and Crafts philosophy. It would be built by local craftsmen using materials such as seasoned oak harvested from the 551-acre estate and limestone gathered from parish quarries. The furnishings for the house were custom-designed down to the smallest detail, from carved blanket chests to inlaid writing desks, all handmade using traditional techniques. The Biddulphs even incorporated a chapel into the house, where a priest conducted daily prayers, anticipating the day when Margaret would retire to a convent. Construction began in 1909 and was completed twenty years later, "a house growing until it finally stood, stately, strong, and bold," wrote one of the Biddulphs' neighbors, the artist William Rothenstein. ¶ As enthusiastic supporters of those traditional crafts endangered by modern technology, the unconventional couple–Margaret, when a debutante, preferred to study landscape architecture than go to tea parties–patronized regional craftsmen and ensured that Rodmarton villagers were trained in traditional techniques to provide them with marketable skills for the future. The hinges for the doors and windows, for example, were made in a purpose-built smithy, the rugs were woven by a disabled farmer, and even the flour for the household's bread was grown and ground on the premises; indeed, most of the produce consumed by the Biddulphs and their staff came from the large kitchen garden and its four greenhouses. Barnsley and his clients conceived the eight acres closest to the manor house as rooms, creating discreet outdoor spaces with individual atmospheres and experiences. The towering hedges and stone walls framed alpine plants in one area and white-flowering plants in another, and the gardens became as renowned as the house in the mid 1950s, when the Biddulphs' son, Anthony, and his wife, Mary, inherited the estate and began adding their own stamp to the place. ¶ Rodmarton Manor, now owned by its builders' grandson Simon Biddulph and meticulously maintained, was as much a vibrant community center as a family home, its sunny, beamed rooms hosting everything from amateur theatrical productions to basket-making classes. The house was less an altruistic folly than it was statement of their shared belief in the artisanal traditions of their country. "I have seen nothing so heartening done in England," Rothenstein recalled, "for here is proof positive that given the opportunity, the old skill and poetry still live under the crust of neglect which covers them."

Gray Foy

Pedestrians cradling iPods and cell phones stroll along the sidewalks outside, but in the rambling, high-ceilinged apartment of the artist Gray Foy in Midtown Manhattan, Queen Victoria still sits on the British throne. Intricate needlepoint is omnipresent; so too is button-tufted upholstery – in the form of a sinuous velvet tête-à-tête, or a Renaissance Revival side chair. Dozens of classic gouaches of Mount Etna erupting hang one above the other in the hall, the fiery volcano eternally belching scarlet lava and smudging the Neapolitan sky with black smoke. Heavy mahogany furniture – a console with a white marble top, a Gothic Revival chair, an opulent sofa carved with bunches of grapes – gleams darkly against walls painted varying shades of purple, the favorite color of Foy's late partner, the legendary editor and indefatigable journal-writer Leo Lerman. ¶ The couple bought widely but with discernment, drawn to what was inexpensive, unfashionable, and evocative of their grandparents' heyday. This might be one reason they settled in the Osborne, a fortress-like apartment house built in 1883 and resembling an Italian palazzo. (The nineteenth century would have welcomed the imposing and extravagantly bearded Lerman, a man with a taste for paisley nightcaps and Verdi operas.) Collections are gathered into themes: the top of an American Empire card table shimmers with iridescent Favrile glass; shelves are dedicated, separately, to treen, horn cups, lacquered boxes from Russia, and polished egg-shaped stones. Tiffany lamps with stained-glass shades illuminate fussy bouquets of flowers composed of delicate seashells. A snowy owl sits under a glass dome, its unblinking stare taking in the horror vacui. No surface has been left unpopulated; as a result there are few places to set a cup or to rest one's hand. Strangely enough, Foy's gemütlich rooms are not suffocating. Although they are densely packed, magnificent order reigns, as does a sense of peace and tranquility.

La Maison Opéra

The splendid but hermetic interiors of Nicole Toussaint du Wast's *hôtel particulier* are not much changed since the architect Charles Garnier designed them in the 1860s. Preserved by triple-curtained windows that keep light at bay, the rooms are repositories of fringed velvet *crapauds*, porcelain vases in the unlikely shape of ruffled pink conch shells, and ponderous mahogany sideboards the size of ancient sarcophagi. Given her vocation as an historian drawn to exaggerated nineteenth-century personalities – such as the tragedienne Rachel and the Bonaparte hostess Laure d'Abrantès – it is appropriate that Toussaint du Wast spent her long life amid the overwhelming splendors of the Second Empire. ¶ Many of the characters whose lives she explored would have been familiar with her family's neo-baroque *hôtel particulier* in Paris, built at the same time as Garnier's masterpiece, the Paris Opéra. Heavily gilded doors gleam as they open and close, catching for an instant the dim light that has managed to slip past the passementeried margins of the thick curtains. Every molding is carved in high relief and finished with gold, so they impress from a distance and glimmer even in the house's eternal shadow. The only flowers that bloom are artful representations – woven into tapestries set into the salon's *boiserie*, in the huge urn that anchors the dining room's towering chimneypiece, and in upholstery held fast by golden nails. Even the vibrant green ferns in the cachepots are false; real ones would be unable to survive the Stygian gloom.

Brodie Castle

‹‹‹‹‹‹‹‹‹‹‹‹‹‹‹‹‹‹‹‹‹ INVERNESS ›››››››››››››››››››››
›››››››››››››››››››››››› SCOTLAND
1986 ::: ‹‹‹‹‹‹‹‹‹‹‹‹‹‹‹‹‹‹‹‹‹

Aficionados of castles can be unsettled by the Scottish variety, examples of which can
sometimes blend brooding battlements and crow-stepped gables with crudely florid plaster
ornamentation and furniture seemingly better suited to a nineteenth-century Paris salon.
At Brodie Castle, east of Inverness–home for eight centuries to a quarrelsome clan that
traces its roots to Pictish tribes–this combination of Highland vigor and Continental
sophistication is particularly affecting, rather like a rough-hewn warrior dressed in dashing,
if slightly ill-fitting, court attire. Fragile Sèvres porcelain figurines and an eighteenth-
century French bombé chest of drawers with delicate ormolu sabots are in sharp contrast
to the vaulted ceiling of the Blue Sitting Room, a plaster arc embossed with irregular
scrolls, rough strapwork, and spiny thistles. Though layers of fashionable improvements
have been made over time to the sixteenth-century fortified tower house, ranging in tone
from neoclassical restraint to Victorian solidity, the castle's robust and hardy soul remains
undiminished. ¶ The honey-colored library, installed in the late nineteenth century,
embodies Victorian propriety, with sturdy oak shelves holding thousands of morocco-bound
volumes, and sunny corners furnished with chairs, tables, and settees for contemplative
study. The drawing room, on the other hand, seems more a setting for a musical comedy,
a comfortable light blue space where flowered chintz meets a candy-red tartan carpet
bought in 1851 at the Great Exhibition of the Works of Industry of All Nations in London.
The castle's theatrical sweep of rooms–each with its own distinct character and historic
atmosphere–seems fitting, considering the last resident of the castle, a laird formally
known as the 25th Brodie of Brodie of that Ilk, had been an actor in his youth.

NYMANS

From leaded windows curtained with flowered chintz to a dressing-table mirror draped in filmy
lace in the manner of the eighteenth century, the serene country-house appearance of Nymans, an idyllic
West Sussex manor famous for its gardens, belies its inspired trickery. The rambling, seemingly medieval
stone structure was actually conceived in the 1920s by Maud and Leonard Messel as an inventive recladding
and expansion of a mediocre Regency villa. "It was not until I was 16 that I realized the house was a complete
fake," the photographer Lord Snowdon, one of the couple's grandsons, once said. Two decades later, fire
swept through the building and left much of the house in ruins. Unruffled by the conflagration, the Messels
simply tidied up the scorched walls and shattered windows and re-invented the gutted, roofless Great Hall as
a picturesque folly, a honeysuckled faux-Gothic backdrop to herbaceous borders, blush-pink apple trees, and
beds of old-fashioned roses. Their daughter, Anne, a celebrated beauty of the 1930s, wryly called the habitable
remains of her childhood home the "potting shed" and, upon inheriting the Tudor revival structure, she and her
husband, the sixth Earl of Rosse, brought a new layer of personality to bear on the plastered and paneled rooms
that had been furnished by her parents and grandparents. Jacobean oak, Italian baroque walnut, and Georgian
satinwood were joined by rumpled slipcovers, floral curtains, and a 1960s television set with a fanciful case
painted by Lady Rosse's brother, the theatrical designer Oliver Messel. ¶ Nymans has been a museum since
1994, but the spell it casts remains reassuringly domestic, an intimate counterpoint to the lavish landscape.
The huge bouquets of wild and cultivated flowers and dramatic grasses that were the countess's hallmark still
enliven the comfortable, low-ceilinged rooms–"She had a way with flowers, and they had a way with her,"
as a friend admiringly observed. More importantly the harmonious jumble of antiques, mended tapestries,
family snapshots, and stacks of *Country Life* are evidence, Lady Rosse wrote, of "the personalities and whims of
those who have trod its paths and the aspirations of its makers and improvers; mirroring a glimpse from each
generation, that time and growth have molded into a harmonious whole."

Umaid
Bhawan Palace

Few patrons of the Art Deco movement were as enthusiastic as some of the twentieth-century maharajahs of India. With a genuine interest in contemporary taste, they commissioned furniture, limousines, houseboats, airplanes, trains, jewels, portraits, and palaces in the latest styles as emblems of their cultural urbanity. One of the most discerning of these Maecenases of the Subcontinent was His Highness Umaid Singhji Sahib Bahadur, penultimate ruler of the princely state of Jodhpur. Partly to pursue his interest in contemporary design and also as a project to provide employment for his people during a prolonged drought, the young maharajah announced that he would build an up-to-date residence for his family, the Rathore dynasty. From 1929 until 1942, more than 3,000 laborers constructed Chittar Palace, now called Umaid Bhawan, a sandstone extravaganza whose pollen-yellow cupola and vaulted interiors give it the appearance, as one visitor observed, of a marriage of "Castle Howard with the Baths of Caracalla." What he thought of the maharajah's private train, gleaming with silvery metal and cushioned in leather, is unknown. ¶ Although the monumental exterior of the 347-room structure draws inspiration from traditional Hindu temples – the architect was an Englishman, Henry Vaughan Lanchester, best known for giving the Welsh city of Cardiff a majestically domed city hall – Umaid Bhawan's soignée interiors are an echoing ode to film-set glamour, their Art-Deco extravagance unmatched anywhere in India. The underground swimming pool is paved with oversized mosaic symbols of the zodiac, and white marble staircases unwind majestically, as if designed to accentuate the slow descent of women in saris. ¶ Sadly, the custom-made lacquer-and-chrome furnishings supplied by a London department store were lost when the ocean liner bearing them to India was sunk by a German submarine. Undaunted, the maharajah and his wife directed a Polish decorator to have it all reproduced by local craftsmen and combine the new furniture with tiger skins, elephant tusks, and nightclub-style murals depicting scenes from Indian mythology – finishing the rooms just in time for a Christmas Eve party a few months later.

CITY PALACE

JAIPUR ○ RAJASTHAN ○ INDIA ○ 1990

An intricate, interlocking progression of opulent mansions, temples, and gardens that has grown
for more than 300 years inside the pink city of Jaipur, the City Palace is an architectural labyrinth.
Each imposing building of this magnificent complex melds into the next, connected by brightly
painted corridors and arcades that provide an escape from the glaring sunlight and lead to cool
shadowed rooms. Colorful marble inlays blossom along the margins of delicate ceremonial arches;
fountains splash in formal courtyards fragrant with marigolds. Set into the rose, yellow, and white
façades of this royal metropolis are thousands of windows, some covered with lace-like screens designed
to obscure the ladies of the harem from the curious gaze of outsiders but still allowing them glimpses of
life beyond the seclusion of the zenana. Although Western touches made fashionable in India in the mid-
twentieth century are everywhere, such as tiered chandeliers of French crystal and club armchairs with moss
fringe (legacies of the beautiful maharani Gayatra Devi, a princess of Cooch Behar), it is the traditional
eighteenth-century Rajasthani aesthetic that dominates. In the columned Hall of Beauty, fragments of mirror
and mica set in finely gilded plaster refract the filtered sunlight and flash the passing of jewel-colored saris
like a giant kaleidoscope. ¶ The days of maharajahs receiving emissaries from far-off lands are history now but
the ebullient head of the Kachwaha dynasty, Sawai Bhawani Singh Bahadur–known as Bubbles for the vintage
Champagne pumped through the City Palace's fountains in celebration of his birth–ensures the atmosphere
of his ancestral domain is unchanged, as if the Indian princely states had not been abolished decades ago.
Garnished with red and green enamel flowers, panels of mirrored glass, and encrustations of dull gold leaf,
one of the maharajah's many sitting rooms, with its divans made of silk cushions arranged at opposite
ends of a fragile Persian carpet, awaits the intimate conversations and languid postures of old.

Chillingham Castle

The present owners of Chillingham Castle – an imposing fortified structure in Northumberland dating from the twelfth century, when it began life as a monastery – Sir Humphry Wakefield, 2nd baronet, and his wife, Katherine, have collected oddments of all styles and eras and assembled them with a blithe and charming disregard for period. Fierce-looking medieval weapons overlook William and Mary chairs; an Irish Georgian table sits near portraits of blushing Regency ladies set in giltwood frames; and modern reproductions of antiques produced through Sir Humphry's association with an American furniture company round out the eclectic decoration. Elk horns surmount the Minstrel's Hall, curious companions to an Arabic banner from the 1898 battle of Omdurman in Sudan, when the 21st Lancers, led by General Sir Herbert Kitchener, triumphed over the soldiers of Caliph Abdullah al-Taashi. The Torture Chamber has all the expected implements of corporal punishment, including thumbscrews and an iron maiden lined with spikes – small wonder the castle is known as one of the most haunted sites in England – while the Plaque Room is hung with paintings depicting the famous Chillingham wild cattle, a rare white breed that have wandered Northumberland since Roman times. ¶ The castle and its gardens, however, look untouched by time. When the Wakefields bought the estate in 1981, it had been left unoccupied for nearly five decades by the earls of Tankerville, who abandoned it to the elements after selling off the slate roof shingles and emptying its rooms of anything remotely valuable. As a result, "the interior has... seen vicissitudes," as Nikolaus Pevsner drily wrote after a visit in the 1950s. Ceilings had fallen in, piles of bat guano caked the rotting plank floors, and much fine wood paneling had disappeared, fed to the fireplaces by Canadian troops who camped here during World War II. The house's condition was so dire that Lady Wakefield, whose ancestors coincidentally had built the castle, declined to visit the property until her husband had made it habitable, a state achieved only after ten years of dedicated labor. Today Chillingham is far more than livable – it has been brought back to life.

Tucked into a cliff in the village of Sidi Bou Saïd, just outside of Tunis, the blinding white palace known as Ennejma Ezzahra, or Star of Venus, is an Orientalist's dream. Windows framed by brilliant blue shutters overlook the Mediterranean, while the cool, marble-floored rooms are decorated with lace-like plasterwork and enriched by banquettes covered in threadbare nineteenth-century velvet. In the library is a chest, reportedly once owned by Suleiman the Magnificent and elsewhere, Chinese ginger jars, Persian prayer mats, and tables—some brass-topped like lily pads, others octagonal and inlaid with mother-of-pearl—fill the rooms.

TUNIS / TUNISIAN REPUBLIC / 1993 ENNEJMA EZZAHRA

Like the nobleman who built it, Baron Rodolphe d'Erlanger, Ennejma Ezzahra is an amalgam of Gallic style, British money, and American industry. A painter, banking heir, and grandnephew of the Civil War general P.G.T. Beauregard, d'Erlanger moved his young family to the French protectorate of Tunisia in 1909, partly for health reasons—bronchitis eventually killed him at the age of sixty—but also to devote his life to studying *ma'luf*, traditional Arab Andalusian music. Its thumping beats and falsetto tones had been ignored by most Western scholars but d'Erlanger became *ma'luf*'s champion and patron and envisioned Ennejma Ezzahra, with its splashing fountains and stone columns, as both residence and concert hall. Completed in 1921 by Moroccan and Tunisian craftsmen, the palace echoed with the sounds of kettle drums, tambourines, and lutes as the baron worked on his six-volume magnum opus, *La Musique Arabe*, and his wife, Bettina, played bridge beneath the elaborately painted wood ceilings of which no two are alike. Preserved today as the Arab and Mediterranean Music Center, Ennejma Ezzahra remains a cultural oasis.

VILLA TAYLOR

Villa Taylor, hailed as the most beautiful house in Marrakech, was the domain of society hostess Madeleine "Boule" de Breteuil from 1946 until her death in 1994. The countess entertained the world in her rose-scented mansion, its dozens of mint green, yellow, and blue chambers lavished with sheepskin carpets, French-country antiques, and pierced-metal lanterns casting shards of light across painted-cedar paneling. During World War II Winston Churchill and Franklin D. Roosevelt briefly took shelter behind the property's high walls after the Casablanca Conference – one of the prime minister's paintings of the Jemaa el Fna, the vast earthen square that is the heart of the old city, still hangs inside. Charlie Chaplin and Rita Hayworth stayed here, too, and at the countess's dinner table could be found numerous members of the international *jeunesse dorée* of the 1960s, such as Talitha Getty and the singer Marianne Faithfull. ¶ Banked with orange and olive trees and threaded around courtyards, the sprawling red-stucco structure was built in 1923 for Edith and Moses Taylor, Rhode Island bluebloods supported by railroad millions. The architect was Henri Prost, an expatriate Parisian known best for his inventive urban planning, yet gifted at creating mansions for Marrakech's expatriate set. His commission for the American couple was especially extravagant, with its marquetry walls and jewel-like painted ceilings rendering it finer even than the admired eighteenth-century palace occupied by the French governor general. The Taylors wintered there for decades, shuttling between continents in the comfort of a 310-foot steam yacht, and called it Villa La Saadia, or the House of Happiness.

Chiswick House

⁂ LONDON ⁂ ENGLAND ⁂ 2008 ⁂

Despite its name, Chiswick House was never meant to be a residence. The eighteenth-century architect and arbiter of style Richard Boyle, the 3rd Earl of Burlington, planned the domed Palladian pavilion near London to be a gallery for displaying his collection of French and Italian paintings and sculptures, while its basement contained his treasured library, home to four original sets of Andrea Palladio's influential 1570 work, *I Quattro Libri dell'Architettura*. Guests would stroll through Chiswick's ornately gilded octagonal saloon and velvet-lined chambers, admiring the earl's acquisitions – among them Roman busts mounted above doors and a copy of Van Dyck's portrait of Charles I and Henrietta Maria – and perhaps taking in the subtle symbols worked into the structure's decoration, both Masonic and Jacobite. Rousseau, Walpole, and Pope sang the temple's praises, and Queen Caroline, consort of George II, reportedly proclaimed it "the prettiest thing I have seen in my life." Lord Hervey, on the other hand, dismissed Chiswick House as nothing more than a charming folly, "too little to live in, and too large to hang to a watch." Eventually the freestanding stucco-faced structure proved to be inconvenient for Lord Burlington to access with ease, so a two-story link was built to connect it with Old Chiswick House, his Jacobean mansion that stood alongside. ¶ An early admirer and proponent of the neoclassical buildings of Palladio, the earl – in partnership with William Kent, the architect and designer, who shared Boyle's passion – created Chiswick House as an adaptation of the Italian architect's masterpiece, Villa Almerico-Capra (often known as La Rotonda) in Vicenza. Its English counterpart, completed in 1729, arguably launched the Palladian movement in Britain and certainly cemented the "Architect Earl's" reputation as Walpole's "Apollo of the Arts." ¶ Seventy years later, Chiswick House became a center of Whig society at the time of Burlington's grandson, the 5th Duke of Devonshire, and his wife, Georgiana, who tore down the Jacobean mansion and added ungainly wings to make Burlington's gallery habitable (these were removed in the 1950s). Later Devonshires found the property to be one house too many and rented it to a surprisingly wide variety of inhabitants, including the future King Edward VII and later to a family of doctors who established a private mental asylum for the affluent.

✛✛

ACKNOWLEDGMENTS

*   *   *

A photographer, particularly one who photographs houses, is dependent on commissions and on the encouragement of editors. As is well known, *Architectural Digest*, in whose pages many of the houses featured in this book first appeared, owes its success to Paige Rense, its Editor-in-Chief. I have been a particular beneficiary of her editorship and owe her an immense debt of gratitude for the confidence she has shown in me, above all in publishing features on houses that at the time might have seemed too unconventional to most other editors, who lacked her vision.

My thanks are also due to all the owners, past and present, of the houses shown in this book and in particular to Tim Knox, director of Sir John Soane's Museum, who commissioned me to photograph the museum and kindly allowed me to use some of those photographs in this book.

In making the selections for *In House* I have missed the guiding eye of Joe Holtzman, whose exceptional vision was of such help in the choice of photographs for *Rooms*. I have been fortunate, however, in Daniel Streat of Barnbrook Design who is mainly responsible for the layout for this book and who has shown great patience in the face of my changes and general neuroses.

I would also like to thank all the people at my laboratory, Resolution Creative, and my editor at Rizzoli, Jacob Lehman, who has been a model of understanding and tolerance throughout the book's gestation.

— *Derry Moore*

✛✛✛✛✛✛✛✛✛✛✛✛✛✛✛✛✛✛